"This generation of Christians inhabit cultures that sometimes reject not only biblical revelation about reality, but also the reality of reality itself. The Questions for Restless Minds series poses many of the toughest questions faced by young Christians to some of the world's foremost Christian thinkers and leaders. Along the way, this series seeks to help the Christian next generation to learn how to think biblically when they face questions in years to come that perhaps no one yet sees coming."

—**Russell Moore,**

public theologian, *Christianity Today*

"Danielle Sallade shows how the Bible challenges our current culture of obsessive busyness and identity fulfillment through work. Danielle demonstrates how we can approach our work from a position that is grounded in Scripture and secure in our primary identity as a servant of Jesus. She is alive to the practical implications for college students, providing many thoughtful reflections to help them consider—and possibly reconsider—what makes their work valuable and meaningful in the sight of God. This book would be helpful to college students who are seeking to understand what God has to say about their academic work and career choices, and also to anyone who works with college students and wants to provide wisdom about spiritually-healthy attitudes and habits related to work."

—**Anna Megill,**

campus minister, Princeton Christian Fellowship

"A bit over two decades ago, I headed to Princeton with a drive to escape the lower middle class and accomplish 'great things,' taking advantage of every opportunity in front of me. It's the kind of setup that could have easily led to 'gaining the whole world' but forfeiting my soul, if not in the eternal sense then in the everyday relinquishment of the peace and abundant life that Jesus has purchased at such great cost. In his mercy, the Lord brought me into the orbit of faithful campus ministers, including Danielle Sallade. And in her book on human flourishing, Sallade winsomely and patiently presses precious truths into the souls of her readers. Finding our identity in the finished work of Christ on our behalf. Mustering up the courage and trust to practice Sabbath. Prioritizing faithfulness over and above worldly productivity. Seeking treasure that can't depreciate. I've passed these words onto numerous young men and women. And I re-read it annually myself, not merely for the incisive cultural analysis but because as a father of five and a bi-vocational pastor, its reminders are always timely. May the Holy Spirit use this book to direct many more hearts to the 'love of God and the steadfastness of Christ.'"

—**Curtis Saxton,**
pastor, Ekklesia of North Philadelphia;
director of analytics, Acelero Learning

# How Do Humans Flourish?

Questions for Restless Minds

**Questions for Restless Minds**

QUESTIONS FOR RESTLESS MINDS

# How Do Humans Flourish?

**Danielle Sallade**

D. A. Carson,
Series Editor

**LEXHAM PRESS**

*How Do Humans Flourish?*
Questions for Restless Minds, edited by D. A. Carson

Copyright 2022 Christ on Campus Initiative

Lexham Press, 1313 Commercial St., Bellingham, WA 98225
LexhamPress.com

Print ISBN 9781683595076
Digital ISBN 9781683595083
Library of Congress Control Number 2021937692

Lexham Editorial: Todd Hains, Abigail Stocker, Mandi Newell
Cover Design: Brittany Schrock
Interior Design: Abigail Stocker
Typesetting: Justin Marr

The Christ on Campus Initiative exists to inspire students on college and university campuses to think wisely, act with conviction, and become more Christlike by providing relevant and excellent evangelical resources on contemporary issues.

Visit christoncampuscci.org.

# Contents

# Series Preface

D. A. CARSON, SERIES EDITOR

THE ORIGIN OF this series of books lies with a group of faculty from Trinity Evangelical Divinity School (TEDS), under the leadership of Scott Manetsch. We wanted to address topics faced by today's undergraduates, especially those from Christian homes and churches.

If you are one such student, you already know what we have in mind. You know that most churches, however encouraging they may be, are not equipped to prepare you for what you will face when you enroll at university.

It's not as if you've never known any winsome atheists before going to college; it's not as if you've never thought about Islam, or the credibility of the New Testament documents, or the nature of friendship, or gender identity, or how the claims of Jesus sound too exclusive and rather narrow, or the nature of evil. But up until now you've probably thought about such things within the shielding cocoon of a community of faith.

Now you are at college, and the communities in which you are embedded often find Christian perspectives to be at best oddly quaint and old-fashioned, if not repulsive. To use the current jargon, it's easy to become socialized into a new community, a new world.

How shall you respond? You could, of course, withdraw a little: just buckle down and study computer science or Roman history (or whatever your subject is) and refuse to engage with others. Or you could throw over your Christian heritage as something that belongs to your immature years and buy into the cultural package that surrounds you. Or—and this is what we hope you will do—you could become better informed.

But how shall you go about this? On any disputed topic, you do not have the time, and probably not the interest, to bury yourself in a couple of dozen volumes written by experts for experts. And if you did, that would be on *one* topic—and there are scores of topics that will grab the attention of the inquisitive student. On the other hand, brief pamphlets with predictable answers couched in safe slogans will prove to be neither attractive nor convincing.

So we have adopted a middle course. We have written short books pitched at undergraduates who want arguments that are accessible and stimulating, but invariably courteous. The material is comprehensive enough that it has become an important resource for pastors and other campus leaders who devote their energies to work with students. Each book ends with a brief annotated bibliography and study questions, intended for readers who want to probe a little further.

Lexham Press is making this series available as attractive print books and in digital formats (ebook and Logos resource). We hope and pray you will find them helpful and convincing.

**1**

# INTRODUCTION

$M$ANY PEOPLE ARE discussing what constitutes genuine human flourishing.[1] One helpful definition comes from theologian Nicholas Wolterstorff, who ties the concept of human flourishing in the Christian tradition to shalom. A flourishing life will be a life lived in right relationship with God, with one's environment, with neighbors, and with self. "A flourishing life is neither merely an 'experientially satisfying life,' as many contemporary Westerners think, nor is it simply a life 'well-lived,' as a majority of ancient Western philosophers have claimed."[2] It is a life that both goes well and is lived well.

I have the privilege through my vocation in campus ministry of serving current university students. My colleagues and I desire for our students to mature in their Christian faith during their college years. We long for them to flourish, borrowing from Wolterstorff, in right relationship with God (through justification in Christ), with their environment (caring for their habitat and working for justice as stewards accountable to God), with their neighbors (showing mercy in the name of Christ and spreading the gospel), and with themselves (proper self-understanding rooted in adoption by God in Christ). As we work toward this goal, we increasingly face challenges from the campus-culture that work against the students' ability to flourish. And one challenge in particular seems to affect everyone: the problem of being too busy.

The students I work with are talented, creative, and intelligent. They are full of energy, working hard in their classes and in various extracurricular activities. They are community-minded, developing friendships, keeping up with family far away, and devoting time to service with genuine care. They are wonderfully inventive about ways to have fun and make memories. But they are also very, very busy. And often because of their "busyness," the students are stressed, anxious, exhausted, and sometimes depressed. The combination of coursework, extracurricular activities, part-time work to cover the ever-increasing cost of their education, and having a social life makes their lives very full with little margin for rest or the unexpected.

In addition, today's students are anxious to realize their personal hopes to "be all they can be," having been taught to expect they could realize this from the beginning of their primary education. They are fearful about their future security, and they struggle to exert as much control over their lives as possible. As a result, they are often suffering from the weight of their various responsibilities and their fears for what lies ahead. Depending on a student's temperament, they can either be caught up in frenzied activity or overwhelmed by their lives and thus unable to do anything. The pressure in their lives keeps them from flourishing as God intended.[3]

This book proposes that living as a Christian, an alternative to the prevailing culture, leads to flourishing. First, I briefly sketch what the worldly culture of busyness looks like. I then discuss how our modern notions about the nature of work and success create the culture of busyness and keep it going. Finally, I attempt to show how the Christian faith offers an alternative way to understand work and success that, when believed and lived out, results in joy, peace, and genuine flourishing instead of stress, anxiety, and exhaustion.

# 2

# THE CULTURE
# OF BUSYNESS

OVERWORK AND OVERCOMMITMENT are very common in student life, to the point of being the normal experience. Academic requirements alone can keep a student working hard through four years. But I have yet to meet a student who simply attends classes and completes the work necessary for those classes. Many students balance academics with paid work necessary to help their parents finance their education and living costs. And education costs have skyrocketed in the last decade. Though some universities can offer financial aid, many cannot, so paying tuition bills takes much hard work and sacrifice for many students.

In addition, it seems that everyone is involved in at least one extracurricular activity where a regular time commitment is necessary for purposeful involvement. This usually means activities on multiple days per week for just one pursuit, and most students are involved in more than one activity. With much to balance, students seem to be constantly on the move, going from personal appointment to class to extracurricular activities to work until the wee hours of the night (many campuses have rehearsals and sports practices that begin at 11 p.m.). The pace of students' lives means that they will skip meals or forsake adequate rest or exercise to be everywhere they are supposed to be and to meet every deadline pressing down on them. "All-nighters" are common.

Changes in technology have also intensified the pace of life. As students move from place to place, they are on their phones or computers, making calls, emailing, or texting one another, making more plans and squeezing it all in. They constantly make and change appointments at the last minute, which intensifies the sense of running around.

Another change brought about by technology is that students now submit assignments electronically. This frees professors to set deadlines for assignments at midnight or 6 a.m. When I was a college student, students had to physically hand in papers that were due during the day or by 5 p.m, the time when the departmental office closed. As a result, this drew a clear boundary between the school day and the evening. Now professors contribute to a "work around the clock" way of life by having middle-of-the-night or weekend deadlines, thereby encouraging students to work at all times. Because work can be accomplished anywhere at any time, students feel pressure to always be working. There is a blurred distinction between day and night, and sleep schedules are often erratic.

After visiting a campus and interviewing students about the nature of college life for today's students, columnist David Brooks observed,

> In our conversations, I would ask the students when they got around to sleeping. One senior told me

that she went to bed around two and woke up each morning at seven; she could afford that much rest because she had learned to supplement her full day of work by studying in her sleep. As she was falling asleep, she would recite a math problem or a paper topic to herself; she would then sometimes dream about it, and when she woke up, the problem might be solved. I asked several students to describe their daily schedules, and their replies sounded like a session of Future Workaholics of America: crew practice at dawn, classes in the morning, resident-advisor duty, lunch, study groups, classes in the afternoon, tutoring disadvantaged kids in Trenton, a cappella practice, dinner, study, science lab, prayer sessions, hit the StairMaster, study a few hours more. One young man told me that he had to schedule appointment times for chatting with friends. I mentioned this to other groups, and usually people would volunteer that they did the same thing. "I just had an appointment with my best friend at seven this morning," one woman said. "Or else you lose touch."[4]

Though Brooks's description is meant to be a generalization and perhaps slight comic exaggeration, it does ring true. The students I regularly meet with lead similar lives.

Living like this, it makes sense that when you ask students what they look forward to the most over their semester breaks, the most common answer is sleep. They push themselves hard, waiting for the time at home when they can "crash" and try to make up for the rest they have missed during classes, only to return and live the same cycle all over again. So much stress is one reason (but certainly not the only reason) that universities have documented a marked rise in the use of counseling services.[5] Members of our university administration have expressed thanks to our ministry because they know that we meet regularly with students throughout each week. They recognize that with the demands for counseling increasing so much in recent years, a ministry like ours is poised on the front lines, helping the university preemptively handle the load.

With negative results like this, one would think that students would stop living without margin. But students take challenging courses and sign up for activity after activity to the point of running ragged because it seems expected. There is a strong sense that everyone is living this way and that if you do not live this way you are either missing out or will not measure up. But if you do live this way, then you will be on the pathway to success.

The story of a recent graduate illustrates this expectation. Back in 2002, our university's alumni magazine published a cover article highlighting a remarkable young woman named Lillian Pierce, the class valedictorian for that year. The article described how Lillian's accomplishments caused her to stand out from among her classmates and even from other valedictorians from past years. She won countless awards for being the outstanding student in her primary departments of math and science, was the first to score perfect scores on many of her tests, maintained an above 4.0 GPA, and won the prestigious Marshall and Rhodes scholarships during her senior year. She was also hailed as one of the best violinists ever to attend the school, serving as the concertmaster for the University Orchestra and performing with professional quartets and orchestras. She made time to tutor in chemistry and math. One of her professors commented that he had never seen a student like her.

After listing these amazing accomplishments, the article goes on to describe the hard work and personal sacrifices Lillian endured to achieve so much. In the article, Lillian is admirably honest and open describing her way of life:

> During her first year at Princeton, says Pierce, "I stopped sleeping. I got so tired that I couldn't eat any more. I was too exhausted to have the motivation to eat. I lived in the infirmary for quite a while. At the same time I was having trouble being with a roommate. I realized I needed privacy if I was going to be able to work as hard as I wanted to. There was one semester sophomore year where I was staying up all night three nights a week. I really felt ill all the time. I had that much work, and I had it every week. I spent the first three years here feeling horrible, it was pretty awful actually. And my hand hurt from writing because sometimes I had to write 40 pages

of math out in one night. It was painful even to keep using the pencil. It wasn't really fun." Despite her exhaustion, she says, when she realized that she was so close to being a good candidate for the Rhodes, "I felt like I couldn't stop." The moment she found out that she had indeed been chosen as a Rhodes Scholar, "I felt I hadn't relaxed in about a decade."[6]

Lillian achieved just about every academic and extracurricular award a student could achieve, but obviously at great cost. Though Lillian's achievements are far above normal, the description of how hard she pushed herself at times is more common.

I remember being amazed when I first read this article that it seemed no one at the university, except those in the infirmary who nursed her when she became ill, counseled Lillian to change her ways. Even though most would agree that she worked too hard and should not have isolated herself from other people to accomplish her work, most nonetheless greatly admired her because of her many awards. By garnering praise and winning awards, Lillian became exalted as an example of achievement for others to emulate. It is no wonder then that students feel pressure to push themselves so hard to achieve.

At this point, we should ask how this culture of overwork has developed. David Brooks writes that students believe "all of the experiences of college life are a step on the continual stairway of advancement, and they are always aware that they must get to the next step (law school, medical school, whatever) so that they can progress up the steps after that."[7] Brooks argues that today's college students have been trained to become professional résumé builders. Higher education, says Brooks, is no longer focused on students' character development or the pursuit of moral wisdom needed to serve society. Instead, it has become a checkpoint to pass through on the way to the ultimate destination of a certain type of job.

Though most students pursue their various interests in part because they genuinely enjoy them, I would agree with Brooks that few seem to do what they do purely for the joy of it. Students think in terms of how their interests help them stand out from others and how their interests will help future employers notice them. And in our culture today, living like this does not begin in college. Students are trained to think of their lives in terms of the résumé they are building much earlier, in junior high and especially high school. The main thing that changes in college is that the lifestyle intensifies as there is more time to fill, often without the boundaries of family life and a parent telling you to go to bed.

Making adolescence (and for some, earlier childhood) a time to begin résumé-building for the future has developed in our society because "admission to a brand-name college is viewed by many parents, and their children, as holding the best promise of professional success and economic well-being in an increasingly competitive world."[8] Because of this viewpoint, the numbers of students applying to colleges all over the country has greatly increased. And getting into a college has become more and more competitive.

Our Dean of Admission at Princeton University highlights this increased competitiveness with recent statistics. She explained that in 1977, the acceptance rate was twenty-four percent of those who applied. In 1993, the acceptance rate was fifteen percent of those who applied, and then in 2007 the acceptance rate was down to 9.7 percent of those who applied, even with that class being the largest in size ever admitted to the school. Thinking of these statistics, the Dean of Admission commented,

> What's hard for families who remember this process from 20 or 30 years ago to grasp is that these candidates today are competing against thousands of other great kids, not hundreds of other great kids. ... Around 10 years ago, we stopped being able to say, "If the student is at this level of qualifications, it's likely that they'll be admitted." It's not likely that anyone in particular will be admitted now. Indeed, last year, 74 percent of the students who applied with SAT scores of over 2300 were not admitted.[9]

And trends like the one described are true of most universities today. Public and private universities all over the country have become more competitive to get into.[10]

The admissions director at Amherst College concludes, "We have now made getting into college the single most important event of a young person's life."[11] The negative result is that some teens in high school are experiencing as much stress as the students I work with in college.

> The new level of competition means that more and more high school students are going to great lengths to stand out. The number of high school students who took Advanced Placement exams in 2004 was 1.1 million, twice as many as in 1994 and six times as many as in 1985. *Time* magazine interviewed Marielle Woods, 17, who participates in twelve extracurricular activities and keeps up a 4.0 average. This can lead to a lot of stress, "always, always before those grades come out, I struggle under a cloud of fear and depression," she says. "Every year I'm silently convinced that this will be the one time I'll actually screw it all up. It's a scary way to live."[12]

My heart goes out to these students because college will be similar in experience without knowing a meaningful alternative.[13]

Just recently, I attended a special celebration of the Fine Arts Day at the school where my young school-age children attend. Their school, which serves pre-K through eighth grade, describes itself as a classical Christian school with a strong Charlotte Mason influence emphasizing learning as the joyful discovery of God's creation. This latter characteristic came through strongly during the whole of the Fine Arts Day, for the students were genuinely excited to be displaying their art work, reciting their favorite poems, and performing all types of music. I was struck by the joy on their faces, their pride in their accomplishments, and their genuine interest in all they had learned.

As I watched the children, I could not help but think of the contrast between what I was seeing there compared to the environment on my campus. I realized that I rarely meet a college student who is so excited about her work that she just can't wait to tell me about her latest discovery in lab or her breakthrough thesis for her literature paper. Once in a while this happens, but when it does, I notice it as unusual. Instead, the students I work with usually talk about their work as something to get done, something to be checked off their long to-do list, something to be worried about. I rarely see students alive with excitement over the joyful discoveries they are encountering in class.

I am troubled by this change in students as they progress through their education, and I have wondered what causes it. I think a major reason behind the change is that college students are constantly thinking about how their education is tied to the job they will get or the graduate school they will apply to. Since they know they are competing for a finite number of jobs or graduate school positions, their focus becomes the competition to outperform everyone else or at least stay toward the top of the pool. Their education and extracurricular pursuits become more about résumé-building and standing out from classmates rather than on what they are learning and how they are enjoying their God-given gifts. The same is true for high school students competing for a finite number of college acceptance letters. This causes pressure, fear, and stress, which in turn causes students to overwork and overcommit.

With this as the environment, my colleagues and I have thought much about how to counsel our students to live out their faith in their unique role as students. What should they believe about the purpose of a college education? How should their faith as Christians affect how they study? How they should manage their time? How should they rest? How might they flourish in the fast-paced, pressure-filled culture they inhabit?

In thinking through the answers to these questions, I have realized that the students' drive to achieve and out-perform others is directly tied to their understanding of the nature of work and their definition of success. Most are working with a worldly viewpoint as their foundation. But as sinners in a fallen world, the worldly viewpoint is flawed and has caused our society to lose a God-centered perspective about work and success. The Bible graciously provides an alternative way to live that is God-centered rather than self-centered. When lived out, the result is freedom from the competitive rat-race and freedom from fear.

Our self-centered rather than God-centered approach has at least three mistakes at its core: (1) We wrongly value certain types of work over others. (2) We place our identity in our work and seek justification through our work. (3) We work as if we were independent operators, solely responsible for our daily provision, forgetting that God is our ultimate provider. These three mistaken perspectives about work affect what people believe about college education, which in turn affects the culture on college campuses today. So the remainder of this book explains these perspectives and contrasts them with a Christian view of work and success. And finally, I discuss the implications of these views for how students should live their daily lives.

## VALUE IN ALL TYPES OF WORK

During World War II, Dorothy Sayers spoke out against the way her society viewed work. She noticed that during the war, people in England were living extremely frugally and sacrificially as everyone came together, working as a team for the war effort. She noticed how different this was from the way people were living right before the war when her society was marked by consumerism, greed, and selfish ambition. As she looked ahead to the time when the war would be over, she challenged her society:

> I ask that [work] should be looked upon not as a necessary drudgery to be undergone for the purpose of making money, but as a way of life in which the nature of man should find its proper exercise and delight and so fulfill itself to the glory of God. That it should, in fact, be thought of as a creative activity undertaken for the love of the work itself; and that man, made in God's image, should make things, as

20

God makes them, for the sake of doing well a thing that is worth doing.[14]

Sayers noticed that during peace time, her society pushed individuals to make the focus of their work making money. So the money-centered individuals became obsessed with spending and investing the monies they earned. But the war forced her society to change by taking the focus in work off of money and placing it on doing things for the society's collective good. Though she wanted the war to end, Sayers did not want to go back to the materialistic way of living that existed before the war.

We can benefit from her critique as well. Our society also reduces work to be a means through which we make money, achieve status, and guarantee personal security. Worldly success is bound up in achievement, but achievements that really matter are ones that produce a lot of money. This is why we wrongly value certain types of work over others. We do not primarily think of our work as a means to serve others or improve society because our focus is so much on compensation with an eye to secure our futures and have plenty of resources to consume in the present.

I see students, and peers for that matter, constantly struggle with misguided notions of what constitutes valuable work. For example, when students are interested in careers that are compensated less than others (say teaching elementary school rather than investment banking), they face a false sense of failure. They might feel that they are not as competent as their peers who will earn more. Or they might feel that they are settling for something less than they are capable of attaining. Parents also contribute to some students' sense of inadequacy because they express disappointment when their son or daughter will be receiving a modest salary or relatively little prestige. (It is common to hear of parents saying to their children, "You want to do what?! I did not send you to university for you to become that!")

I am currently serving a student whose dream job is to work for a national nonprofit organization that exists to serve people with disabilities. But in choosing this path, she continues to deal with criticism from her parents and friends that the proposed salary is not high enough. It is hard for her to remember how her future job so well suits her gifts, past experience, and interests and will also enable her to dedicate her life to serving other people because those around her are pushing her to think about money and status and to value those things above all else. Her story is not unique.

## VALUE IN ALL TYPES
## OF WORK—BY DESIGN

The Bible sets forth the dignity and inherent goodness of all kinds of work and corrects our misguided beliefs that the only work that is valuable is work that earns a lot of money or prestige. First, the creation account in Genesis teaches that work has value because God designed it to be an important way that we image and glorify him—not glorify ourselves. The Genesis narrative explains that God created the world out of nothing. The Spirit of God hovered over the chaos and brought form to the void. Then God filled the form with all kinds of creatures. As God worked, designing each part of the creation, he repeatedly declared that his work was good. Finally, as the pinnacle of creation, he created humans and lovingly set them in paradise to "work and take care of" the creation. Commenting on Genesis 1:26–28, pastor John Piper writes,

> God made man in his own image so that he would be seen and enjoyed and honored through what man does.
>
> Then he [God] said, first of all, that what man does is work. He subdues and takes dominion over the earth. This implies that part of what it means to be human is to exercise lordship over creation and give the world shape and order and design that reflect the truth and beauty of God. God makes man, so to speak, his ruling deputy and endows him with God-like rights and capacities to subdue the world— to use it and shape it for good purposes, especially the purpose of magnifying the Creator.[15]

As we work, we take what God has already created, the raw materials of our world, and we bring forth all that is needed for human flourishing. As years go by, we not only work with the raw materials of our world, but we also work with the cultural products of previous generations. Such cultivation and creativity is found in all kinds of work, from farming to medical arts, engineering, teaching, business, and cleaning. They all have something in common: bringing order, purpose, and form to our world for the benefit of humanity. And work in its variety of forms glorifies God because it mirrors our working God to the world.

God is glorified by all the works of his creation (Ps 19:1–2). But humans have a unique role in bringing glory to God through our work because we are morally conscious and can make choices about our work. Again, Piper writes,

> No beaver or bee or hummingbird or ant consciously relies on God. No beaver ponders the divine pattern of order and beauty and makes a moral choice to pursue excellence because God is excellent. No beaver ever pondered the preciousness and purpose of God and decided for God's sake to make a dam for another beaver and not for himself. But humans have all these potentials, because we are created in God's image. When God commissions us to subdue the earth—to shape it and use it—he doesn't mean do it like a beaver. He means do it like a human, a morally self-conscious person who is responsible to do his work intentionally for the glory of the Maker. ... Therefore, the essence of our work as humans must

be that it is done in conscience reliance on God's power, and in conscious quest of God's pattern of excellence, and in deliberate aim to reflect God's glory.[16]

This teaches us that how we work is as important as what we produce. God is glorified by work because we can do it with an eye to please him.

It is also necessary to remember that our life's work includes more than what we are paid for doing. The Scriptures never limit "work" in this way. For example, the woman of noble character, described in Proverbs 31, is praised for her work in many spheres of life. She is an example first and foremost because her work is rooted in her fear of God (v. 30). She is then praised because of her business dealings and real estate ventures (vv. 16, 24). In today's thinking, we would limit her work to these matters because she is paid for them. But work is more broadly defined as how waking hours are spent when not experiencing Sabbath rest. So the Proverbs 31 woman is equally held up as an example of wise living because of how she manages her household, serves the poor, and instructs her children (vv. 15, 20, 26). All of these areas constitute her work, and all are important. Remembering this would greatly bless those who exclusively work at home, running a household with its many demands, who do not get compensated. It would help level the playing field between paid work and volunteer work, which in turn would help keep us from giving too much time to either one, knowing it is not the only legitimate work we do.

## VALUE IN ALL TYPES OF WORK—BY EXAMPLE

There is another insight into the Genesis creation account that shows forth the dignity of all kinds of work.[17] This insight makes the Genesis account seem radical in its teaching when compared to other worldviews and what they teach about work. Let me explain. The ancient Babylonian creation account, the Enuma Elish, describes the world as created out of a divine conflict. Humanity was then created as an afterthought to worship the gods and work for them. In other words, work is hard, the gods need time off, so enter humanity to do the "bad" work.

Moreover, dualistic worldviews such as Greek and Roman thought regard the world of the mind as superior to the physical realm. Because manual labor is part of the physical realm, they consider it base and avoid it. So in Greek mythology, when Pandora's box opens and looses all evils into the world, work is among them. Roman philosophers repeatedly asserted that only slaves should do manual labor.

Now consider God in the creation account in Genesis. We see him creating with purpose and design, calling his work good. We see that he created humans with great thought and lovingly designed them to be the pinnacle of creation, not as an afterthought like the Babylonian creation account. All work, including physical work, has dignity because God does it. We forget that the first human in Scripture to be filled with the Spirit of God was a craftsman named Bezalel, who was set apart to oversee the construction of the tent of meeting (Exod 31). Would we have rightly valued him today? I fear not.

As pastor Tim Keller has noted, when our Savior came to earth, he did not come as a philosopher (a job the Greeks would have highly valued), nor as a noble statesman (a job the Romans would have highly valued), nor as a powerful military general (a job the Jews would have highly valued), but he came as a carpenter—in our modern lingo, a union guy—and this was the one who would save the world. Thus, we would do well to get rid of our modern notions that only some work has dignity because of the compensation and prestige that go with it. We should stop thinking that some work is less valuable because it pays less, requires less education, and is physical in nature rather than cerebral.

Rightly valuing all types of work would encourage students to assess their unique gifts, interests, education, and family needs and pursue future employment based on connecting these individual traits to the service of others. Students (and their parents) would be willing to consider the many fields today that need more qualified workers as good options. They would stop trying to fit themselves into certain careers, whether their gifts lead them that way or not, because of the lure of money or prestige. They would be free to think about how their work can glorify God and bless others.

Another benefit from rightly valuing all types of work connects to the fact that most students will one day become parents. So many people, and especially women, struggle when they finish years of education, work in a particular job for a time, and then leave their jobs to stay home to parent small children and run their households. Many wrestle with a deep sense that when they do this, they are throwing their lives away. They cannot appreciate that the different work of running a household and caring for those who cannot care for themselves is legitimate and valuable work.[18] They cannot grasp the notion that the work for their family, which does not bring in a paycheck, might even be more important than what they were doing before. Our hierarchy of work has destructive implications in many directions, family life included.

Let us value work as God intends.

**3**

# IDENTITY
# IN WORK

$A$ SECOND IMPLICATION OF our self-centered approach to work is that work has become the means through which we craft our personal identity. For centuries past, humans found their primary identity in their family and attendant relationships. But now, our culture has shifted the locus of personal meaning from family to our work. Thus, deciding what you will be as a worker and attaining that position is of the utmost importance.[19] This is why it is so common to meet someone for the first time and ask, "What do you do for a living?" Looking back over human history, this is a new way of living.

Os Guinness traces this shift back to the Industrial Revolution. At that time, Guinness explains, the use and definition of the word "calling" shifted from a scriptural understanding (where humans are not called primarily to an occupation or a place, but to a person, Jesus Christ) to a worldly view (calling became synonymous with one's occupation). Thus, one's work became everything. Work even took over from the sacred as the locus of meaning. Proof of this is quotations by those in power: in 1920s-America, business leader Henry Ford asserted, "Every thinking man knows that work is the salvation of the human race, physically, morally, and spiritually." And

President Calvin Coolidge said, "He who builds a factory builds a temple, and he who works there worships there."[20]

When we let our work define us, so much is at stake every time we face a deadline or start a new project because our performance becomes the very measure of our worth. Living this way causes tremendous pressure. The Academy Award winning film *Chariots of Fire* helpfully illustrates this point. One of the characters, an Olympic athlete named Harold Abrahams, looked to his performance as a runner to provide meaning for his life. In a scene before one of his important races, Harold shares his fears: "I will raise my eyes and look down that corridor, four feet wide, with ten lonely seconds to justify my existence. But will I?" In this scene, Harold admits that if he loses, then he is nothing. Running is his life, and if something goes wrong with his running, he is a failure. He must live under the tremendous pressure to be the best.

But there is more. At another point in the film, Harold admits, "I've known the fear of losing, but now I am almost too frightened to win." After years of training and sacrifice to qualify for the Olympics, it makes sense that he would be afraid of losing. But why is he so afraid to win? The answer raises our awareness to the emptiness of achievement for achievement's sake. If all there is to life is personal achievement, then one can never stop achieving to derive meaning. One must perform and keep performing, setting a new goal the moment another is attained, thereby constructing meaning for life. Harold seems to sense the drudgery of such a way of life. He questions, "Is this what life is really about?"

Students today, like many adults, certainly labor anxiously under this notion of personal peace and identity being wrapped up in what they do and what they achieve. I have counseled many students who genuinely fear that their lives are over, so to speak, because of a failing grade on an exam or an injury that sidelines them from their sports season. Who they are has become so tied in to what they do.

This makes sense. Humans long for meaning in their lives. There are many who assert that humans are here by chance, the result of evolutionary mechanisms working in nature, and thus without higher reason for our existence. From this perspective, humans must create their own meaning, and one way people do this is through their achievements. Additionally, many people experience a lingering sense of guilt that drives them to earn approval through perfectionism or through attaining goals at work (checking off all the boxes on a to-do list actually makes people feel good). These very real emotions motivate people to seek ultimate satisfaction in achievement through work, which leaves people empty. Work was not meant to bear such burdens.

## IDENTITY IN CHRIST

Jesus promised his followers that by trusting in him they would know the truth and the truth would set them free. What would it set them free from? The answer is slavery to sin in all of its forms, including the sin of self justification through work. As Christians, the antidote to our restlessness of soul is resting in the truth that we are no longer enemies of God and objects of wrath. Instead, God fully approves and loves us because of Christ's work on our behalf. We have peace with God and access to his glorious throne of grace to find help in our times of need. This changed status provides genuine peace in our lives.

With identity in Christ, we do not have to prove ourselves through work because the only one whose opinion ultimately matters has approved us! Our meaning in life is rooted in the dignity of our image-bearing through creation and in our union with Christ through our redemption. This is why Christians can rest physically (from actual work) and emotionally (from that nagging inner voice that says we are not measuring up) with a deep rest of the soul. We do not need to look to our work or to those we work for to determine our self-worth. As pastor Tim Keller has commented, because Christ said "It is finished" when he labored on the cross, suffering to atone for our sin, God looks at our lives when we put our faith in Christ and says "It is good." We look to Christ, who has lavished his love upon us and set us apart for himself, and we find joy and peace in our beloved status.

With confidence in our right standing with God, our work becomes what God meant it to be—a way to serve God by serving our neighbors. Reformer Martin Luther wrote extensively on the topic of work.[21] Luther argued that all vocations, except those based on clear examples of sin like usury, are valuable to God. Since the gospel alone brings us heaven, humans can stop thinking that religious occupations are more holy than secular ones. Our work enables us to participate in God's ongoing work of creation through our various positions, but this cooperation neither defines our identity nor merits our salvation. If we embrace these truths, we can relax in our work and not look to our performance or type of work either to define us or move us closer to God.

## WORK THAT FLOWS OUT
## OF IDENTITY IN CHRIST

Though we are free from stress by not depending on our work for how we feel about ourselves, following Christ calls us to have a new motivation for God-honoring work. We have a new identity in Christ, who saves us from slavery to sin to become his slaves.[22] Christ has purchased us with his blood (1 Pet 1:18–21; 1 Cor 6:19–20) and has set us free from bondage to sin (Rom 6:19). But once freed from sin, we are still slaves. We become slaves to Christ, but it is a slavery that leads to our freedom and our flourishing because through it we receive the benefits of ever increasing holiness and ultimately eternal life (Rom 6:22–23). So as slaves of Christ, our work for him is not a great burden, nor do we fear our Master. Instead, we work for Christ with great zeal and joy because of all that he has done for us. And we work willingly because he is a Master always working for the good of his slaves.

As I mentioned earlier, all of us have experienced meeting someone new who asked us, "What do you do for a living?" Whenever I hear this question, I immediately think of the apostle Paul. Paul frequently introduced himself in his letters (and I imagine in person as well) as a "slave of Jesus Christ" (Rom 1:1; Phil 1:1). Paul's union with Christ defined his identity and purpose more than the specifics of his work—whether his missions work, his church-planting, his writing, or his top-notch education. Though we do not share Paul's special apostolic calling, we are fellow disciples. Following his example, it is appropriate for us to keep "slave to Jesus Christ" foremost in our minds as what defines us.

Being a slave of Christ changes how we think about our work. Our primary purpose as a slave is extending Christ's kingdom. And when our main focus in life is our duty to Christ, we are free from being overly preoccupied with our specific jobs. For example, we still value our jobs because we recognize that God provided them to supply our needs for food, shelter, and clothing. We still value our jobs as the unique realm in which we work for the kingdom of God to redeem our culture, so we take great care to find work that fits our unique interests and gifts.[23] Our job is a context in which we work for Christ's kingdom, but as Christ's slave, it is more important how we work in our various jobs than what our job actually is.

In the Sermon on the Mount, Christ commands his disciples not to be concerned primarily with food and clothing but rather with righteous living and kingdom-work, confident that their loving heavenly Father will take care of daily needs and free them to seek first his righteousness (Matt 6:25–34). Christ clearly wants our minds free from daily worries so that we can focus on laying up treasure in heaven through obeying his commands. Again, after miraculously feeding 5,000 followers in John 6, Christ exhorts his disciples that their purpose in life is to labor for food that does not perish (believing in Christ and obeying Christ's commands) rather than labor for the food of daily provision that does perish (v. 27). Without needing to worry about daily provision (money, for most of us), we are free to make choices that exalt Christ. So workers are free to act with integrity at the workplace even if it means losing a job because they know that God will provide. Students are free to set limits on the time they study in order to nurture relationships and serve other people because they know that God will provide.

And again, the parable of the talents in Matthew 25 reminds us of the same focus in our work. In the parable, three slaves represent Christ's followers, and the master represents Christ. The master commends two of the slaves because they take his resources (differing amounts in each case) and double them, but he judges and condemns the third slave because he makes excuses and does nothing with the master's resources. This story reminds us that we are slaves of Christ who must be devoted to increasing our Master's assets and extending our Master's kingdom.[24] How do we do this? By obeying Christ's commands in everything we do, whether in small matters or important matters. So we work at our jobs with integrity. We give of our resources gladly. We love our neighbor and we love our enemies. We are devoted to sharing the gospel in our classes, workplace, dorms, and neighborhoods. And the list goes on. Our focus in our work is not maximizing our own resources, but maximizing our Master's.

The parable of the talents also emphasizes that Christ takes great joy in us as we work for him. And then he shares his joy with us so that we too are filled with joy in our kingdom-work. Christ says to the first two slaves, who have doubled the resources, "Come and share in your master's happiness" (Matt 25:21, 23). In the *Nature of True Virtue*, Jonathan Edwards teaches that unless you have experienced the grace of God in your life, self-interest will to some degree drive everything you do. But when you know that God has embraced you fully in Christ and lavishly loves you, then you can do everything for the sheer joy of pleasing Christ.[25] Rooting your identity in Christ and staying focused on your job as Christ's slave causes flourishing because it releases you from anxiety and stress and because you know that the Master promises to provide for your needs. And then it brings great joy and satisfaction as the Master is pleased and shares his joy. How different this is from the agony of soul and intense pressure that comes when we look to our work to define us or prove our goodness. Let us root our identity in Christ and not in our work.

**4**

# DEPENDING
# ON GOD IN
# OUR WORK

$A$ THIRD NEGATIVE EFFECT of our self-centered view of work is how we forget that God is our provider. We believe that our daily provision (through our pay checks) and our future security (through our savings and financial planning) are all a result of our work alone. We forget that every breath we take and every morsel of food we eat comes from the gracious hand of God (Ps 104:27; Matt 6:25–33; Heb 1:3; Jas 1:17). When we think that it is all up to us to provide our daily bread, we open ourselves up to much stress and anxiety. And challenging circumstances intensify this all the more, such as our current recession when jobs are hard to come by and paychecks are downsizing.

Students experience the same stress because they believe so much is on the line as a result of their grades and their résumé-building. They feel like they must overwork because they believe that good grades can guarantee the right job, which can guarantee future security, approval from parents, etc. Students that I know frequently admit the intense pressure they feel to excel in all they do. And they work as if their efforts alone determine all their success today and security tomorrow.

We must remember that we were not meant to live independently from our Creator. From the opening pages of Scripture, God teaches us that he want us—his creatures—to depend on him. As we live in right relationship with him, he graciously promises to provide everything we need. God made us to work for his glory by relying on him to enable our work and provide our daily needs.

Sin causes humans to live independently from God (both actively, insisting there is no God, and passively, simply forgetting he is with us). The story of Babel in Genesis 11 highlights these sinful tendencies. At Babel, humans used their work to gain independence from God. Through their many gifts—gifts for architecture, engineering, and city-planning among them—the people of Babel sought to make a name for themselves rather than making a name for God. And through their work, which would keep the people in Babel together, they expressly disobeyed God's command to fill the earth. They forgot the truth, expressed years later in a psalm of Solomon, that "unless the LORD builds the house, the builders labor in vain" (Ps 127:1). God clearly judged them because humans were not meant to live this way.

The story of how God provided for the infant nation Israel when they were wandering in the wilderness also illustrates God's care for his people and his desire for them to depend on him. At the beginning of their time in the wilderness, God had set the pattern of six days of work followed by one day of rest, modeled after his work in creation. But God had not yet commanded Sabbath-keeping through the Ten Commandments that he later gave at Sinai. At that time, the Israelites grumbled for food, some even longing to go back to Egypt because the prospects in the desert looked so grim. God lovingly and miraculously provided manna, and he provided it in a way that teaches an important lesson about his character and about the meaning of the Sabbath.

Through the daily appearance of manna, God showed the Israelites that they could trust him to take care of their needs. Then on the sixth day, God asked the Israelites to collect enough manna for two days so that they could observe a Sabbath day of rest from work. It was as if God was saying, "Trust in me for today's provision and tomorrow's. I will provide for your daily bread, and I will take care of your anxieties for your future well-being."[26] How we so easily forget that God provides for us. And this is one reason that God commanded Sabbath-observance at Sinai. He knew how easy it would be for his people to forget that he is the one providing. Ceasing from work one day a week would be a tangible reminder of where they were placing their trust—on their own work or on their gracious God.

Consider also Christ's teaching in Luke 12 that calls us to depend on him. First, through the parable of the rich fool (vv. 13–21), Jesus reminds us that no one knows when life will end. The rich fool in the parable has stored away his wealth, tearing down existing barns to build larger ones to hold his vast amount of grain. Then he sits back to take life easy and be merry. Jesus calls him a fool, informs him that he will die that very night, and pointedly asks, "Who will get what you have prepared for yourself?" The rich fool has wasted his life hoarding his wealth for himself and failing to lay up treasure in heaven. At the heart of this mistake is the rich man's self-reliance. He did not take care of others with his resources because he viewed his money as his own, earned by himself and for himself. When we remember that our provision is God's in the first place, it is easy to share generously. But the rich fool forgot that God gave him his personal talents and blessed his hard work with overflowing abundance. He lived independently from God.

Right after Jesus startlingly warns those who are not rich toward God, he tremendously comforts his followers (Luke 12:22–34). This is just what they need to hear because Jesus knows it will take trust to give rather than store up, to look to God for security rather than personal striving. In this next passage, Jesus commands his followers to stop worrying, reminding them that they cannot even do the very little thing of adding one hour to their lives through their worry (though haven't we all wished for one more hour before an exam to keep cramming?). When obeyed, the command to stop worrying brings freedom because of the one making the command. Jesus teaches that we are not alone. Our gracious Father is caring for us, loving us, and providing for us, and he knows our needs and is pleased to give us his kingdom.

I love how Jesus, the Great Shepherd, addresses his followers here as "little flock." He echoes the way God spoke to Israel hundreds of years before: "Do not be afraid, you worm Jacob, little Israel, do not fear, for I myself will help you," declares the Lord, your Redeemer, the Holy One of Israel" (Isa 41:14).[27] This brings forth confidence in God because he is our King, sovereignly controlling our world and powerful enough to provide for us even when our circumstances are grim. And it brings forth trust that we can rest in the loving arms of our Great Shepherd. We can experience peace in our work when we depend on God.

## SABBATH

God made us to work, but we must remember that God is with us in our work, standing behind us as our provider. Again, Psalm 127:1–2 says,

> Unless the LORD builds the house,
>     the builders labor in vain.
> Unless the LORD watches over the city,
>     the guards stand watch in vain.
> In vain you rise early
>     and stay up late,
> toiling for food to eat—
>     for he grants sleep to those he loves.

We are spinning our wheels needlessly when we work as if we are alone in this world, solely responsible for our daily bread, solely responsible for success in our work. We ignore the Lord to our peril, bringing stress and anxiety into our lives.

Recently, a student confessed that he rarely sleeps and had begun to take great pride in his abilities to be awake for twelve hours, sleep for fifteen minutes (a power nap), and keep going, knowing he is doing so much more than other students around him. He is realizing now that those whom God loves are meant to sleep in peace because they have sought God's direction in work and can recognize his sovereignty over the work.

I believe we would be greatly aided in living out our actual dependence upon God (which, like the Israelites in the wilderness, we all too easily forget) if the body of Christ today would make Sabbath-keeping a priority. Most of the Christian students I work among and most of my Christian peers do not take an intentional Sabbath, nor have they been taught much theology undergirding the practice of Sabbath-keeping. And one reason is that our society as a whole has lost any notion of one day a week being set apart for something different than all the rest (with all stores and entertainment venues open, recreational sports leagues in full swing Saturday and Sunday, etc., so that our societal striving and consuming continues seven days a week). Many students attend a service on Sunday morning, but the rest of the day is for school work. On our campus the libraries are the most crowded on Sunday, with Saturday being taken up by social events and extracurricular activities. So outside of the time spent in a service, the cycle of hard work and maxed-out activity does not stop.

For students who are preparing for an unknown career in an unknown place, it is such a challenge not to think that you have to work hard to craft your future by working in the present. But with a weekly day of rest, we can take the focus off of ourselves and place it back, rightfully, on God. Marva Dawn writes,

> In our twentieth-century spirituality we easily lose the notion of God's provision for us because of our advanced civilization and its distance from the actual processes that provide material goods. A major blessing of Sabbath keeping is that it forces us to rely on God for our future. On that day, we do nothing to create our own way. We abstain from work, from our incessant need to produce and accomplish, from all the anxieties about how we can be successful in all that we have to do to get ahead. The result is that we can let God be God in our lives.[28]

We can train ourselves, like the Israelites feeding on manna, to be confident that God is providing for us today and will surely provide for us tomorrow.

Attending a worship service on our Sabbath-day also reminds us that our identity is rooted in Christ and not in our work. As Marva Dawn explains, "In our culture, which attaches such a grand importance to work and productivity, our weekly ceasing reminds us that the value of work lies not in itself, nor in the worth it gives us, but in the worship of God that takes place in it."[29] So worship lifts our gaze toward God and reveals our sins that we let creep into our work. And we can recommit ourselves to working with God and for God as the new week begins. Corporate worship on the Sabbath also brings us into physical contact with our other family members in the body of Christ. So we are visibly reminded of our place in the community and our responsibility for helping take care of the needs of those around us. Again, our focus is drawn outward and we can see the sins of self and repent.

Sabbath-keeping does not have to be rigidly observed on Sunday. Rather, the point is to cultivate a weekly time of rest, which includes ceasing from work and worship of God as a pattern of life. Those who are involved in ministry know that Sunday can be one of the busiest work days of the week. Many ministers pick another day of the week to observe their Sabbath rest (e.g., the church office at my church is closed on Mondays). Other careers (e.g., nursing) or many life circumstances (e.g., caring for an infant or a sick loved one) can involve work through the weekend. So what matters is carving out another time to rest and worship (and I use the word "carving" because it will take thought and intention to create this space in your life).

It will take courage for a student to observe a weekly Sabbath. Students who choose Sabbath rest will see other students studying and working hard for the week ahead and will be tempted to work like everyone else. Those ceasing from work will have to remind themselves that God is with them in their studies and is working on their behalf for their future, so they can trust him by not going to the library. Some students will likely fall behind their peers who press ahead every day of the week, and they will have to make peace with this reality. Embracing this weakness and making room for God to show forth his strength in their lives will be hard. So I recommend that students ask for encouragement and accountability from their peers to press on in their Sabbath-observance because it will be much easier to keep a Sabbath if there are other believers to keep a Sabbath with. But I think the tremendous benefits of peace, trust in God, and growth in serving others will be worth the challenges.

## FOCUS ON FAITHFULNESS

How we view work and how we rest is inevitably tied to what we believe constitutes success. How does our faith shape our definition of success? Usually, our worldly notions of success are tied to money or fame or achieving something no one else has achieved before in a particular field. For example, we admire (and greatly compensate) Alex Rodriquez and Brett Favre for being an MVP in their respective sports even though we may cheer for a different team. We admire Sandra Day O'Connor, Nancy Pelosi, and Hillary Clinton for being the first women to hold their political offices even though we might disagree with their particular viewpoints. We admire Nobel Prize winners in economics, math, and physics even when we cannot understand the nuances of their groundbreaking discoveries. The point is that we often confer greatness because of achievements that we can clearly see, measure, and then reward. In contrast, the Scripture removes our focus from this worldly success and urges us to value faithfulness to God through obedience to Christ as real success. Sharing the Scripture's definition of success can transform how we work.

Consider again how in the parable of the talents in Matthew 25, Christ commends the first two slaves. This demonstrates God's definition of success. When the first slave turns five talents into ten and the second turns two talents into four, Jesus praises them with identical words: "Well done good and faithful servant! You have been faithful with a few things; I will put you in charge of many things. Come and share your master's happiness!" (Matt 25:21, 23). Christ blesses these two slaves because they worked faithfully while their master was away. Contrary to what we might expect, he does not offer more praise for the first slave than he does for the second even though the first expanded more of his resources. No, he values them both equally because they were faithful in their respective stewardship. But Christ condemns the third slave because he was not faithful. So this parable shows us that we should value faithfulness to Christ, expressed through obeying his commands, above everything else we measure our lives by.

When my husband and I were attending seminary, we learned a valuable lesson about success defined as faithfulness from an Old Testament course on the historical books of the Bible.[30] I would like to briefly share with you some of the things we learned about King Omri, the ninth king of Israel, who reigned about 900 years before Christ, because his life illustrates God's definition of success. Most

Christians have heard about King Saul or King David or David's son, King Solomon, and can tell you some details about these kings. But most people, myself included at the time of my course, know little about King Omri. And yet King Omri was arguably, by our world's standards, one of the greatest kings of Israel.

The record of Omri's reign in Scripture is brief, only seven verses found in 1 Kings 16:21–27. Looking at these verses carefully, you can discover that one of Omri's accomplishments was bringing political stability to a nation torn apart by a civil war. He brought much needed peace within the nation for twelve years. He also strengthened Israel's defenses against invading armies, and he defeated Moab, a longtime enemy of Israel going back to the days of Moses. This latter point we also learn about from archaeological records. An archeologist discovered an Assyrian obelisk that bears an inscription referring to Omri as a great warrior and to Israel as the house of Omri. To illustrate this point, New York's Yankee stadium is called "the house that Ruth built" because of the many championships that Babe Ruth led. In like manner, the Assyrians of that time called Israel "the house that Omri built" because of the rise in power Israel experienced under Omri's reign.

Economic prosperity also characterized Omri's reign. He moved the capital of Israel to Samaria, which improved trade and increased foreign commerce. His economic plan put Israel on a path of growth that lasted for the next 200 years. When Amos prophesied to Israel years later, he denounced how materialistic and greedy the nation had become. Much of Israel's rise in wealth began under Omri's reforms.

When taking our course, we imagined Omri running for reelection in our country today. A campaign speech in our modern lingo could have included the following: (1) I spearheaded efforts ending partisan factions that were destroying our country, something all of my predecessors failed to do; (2) I designed an economic package that increased employment and put more money in the pockets of ordinary people; (3) I secured our borders from the ongoing threat of terrorism, keeping our children and loved ones safe in their own homes and communities; (4) I reestablished our country as a respectable and credible force in the eyes of the nations around us. Clearly, Omri did many great things according to how we measure greatness. His picture would have graced the cover of many a magazine.

But what is God's assessment of Omri—this man who achieved much and was great in the eyes of many people? God assesses him in 1 Kings 16:25: "But Omri did evil in the eyes of the LORD and sinned more than all those before him." Omri's greatness was capable of solving many of Israel's social, military, political, and economic problems. But Omri did nothing to solve Israel's most desperate problem: her spiritual sickness. In fact, according to 1 Kings 16:26, Omri only added to the depth of Israel's spiritual sickness: "He followed completely the ways of Jeroboam son of Nebat, committing the same sin Jeroboam had caused Israel to commit, so that they aroused the anger of the Lord, the God of Israel, by their worthless idols." The king of Israel was supposed to be a spiritual leader, reading God's law to the people, living it, trusting in and loving the gracious God who gave the law. But Omri was not interested in these things. His heart turned away from God and trusted other idols, leading others into idolatry as well.

For God, all those great things Omri achieved meant little because Omri's heart was far from God and loving him. So King Omri and the details of his reign occupy only eight verses in 1 Kings 16. Contrast that with a story recorded in the very next chapter: an unnamed Gentile widow and the story of her trust in Israel's God occupies eighteen verses (1 Kgs 17:7–24), and Jesus mentions her at the beginning of his ministry (Luke 4:25–26). This demonstrates God's definition of greatness. God values faithfulness to himself above all else that we might value, and all of Scripture testifies that faithfulness to God is what makes us great in God's eyes.

Earlier in this book, I mentioned the movie *Chariots of Fire*, which contrasts the life of Eric Liddell with fellow athlete Harold Abrahams. The last we see of Eric in the movie, he has won a gold medal and has become a national hero. What the movie does not show is that Eric goes on to be a missionary in China—returning "home," so to speak, having been born in China to British missionary parents. Eric delayed his departure for China to participate in the Olympics and other track and field competitions, but throughout his time of athletic competition, he yearned to go back. So just one year after earning Olympic gold, he moves to China and begins teaching and spreading the gospel.

Unfortunately, in China, Eric's life is cut short in part because of the outbreak of World War II. With many other British citizens, he ends up in a Japanese war camp. He lives in the camp and serves his fellow prisoners there for a few years, but he dies in the camp in 1945, just months before liberation. He was only forty-three years old, and people all over the world mourned for him.

From a worldly perspective, we might think that Eric wasted his life and tremendous gifts. But Eric's faithfulness to the Great Commission and his willingness to sacrifice himself for it are what make him a hero of faith. The fact that his life and ministry ended sooner than others does nothing to change that. This turns our typical way of thinking on its head. It allows us to be gracious to ourselves, realizing that if we are faithful to God in whatever circumstances he has placed us in, then we are successful. It isn't about our money, our fame, our achievements, or the results of our work, but our faithfulness to our God in all we do. How different Israel under King Omri's reign might have been had Omri been fully faithful to God. How differently we might work if we embraced this as well.

**5**

# CONCLUSION

I BEGAN BY DESCRIBING the busyness of student life and the tremendous pressure upon students today to stand out through their achievements to secure a certain type of job. I argued that wrong ideas about work and success drive this pattern of living and enslave students (and workers) to a way of life that is full of high levels of stress, anxiety, and sometimes depression. To close, let me briefly describe a few more implications of living out a God-centered understanding of work and success for college students.

Students who are confident that God values all types of work are most concerned in their education with developing their interests and gifts, learning how they can best channel both of them to serve others and redeem culture. They do not focus on money or prestige, but on stewarding well their God-given abilities and education, because they know that our world needs all type of workers. They do not feel ashamed if they realize that God has gifted them for a lower-paying job. They do not believe that they are throwing their lives away to take on the work of parenting, homemaking, or nursing an ailing loved one.

Students who serve Christ as their primary focus know that how they work with integrity and excellence is more important than the measured results of their work. This frees them to focus as much on being a witness in their classes as excelling in those classes. These students have courage to lay down personal ambition and stop studying in order to serve a friend in crisis the night before an exam. They view their extracurricular interests not just as one more thing to build up their résumé, but as a way for God to use their interests to put them near other people with the same interests for the sake of building relationships for Christ.

As these students pursue their careers, they focus on laying up treasure in heaven through their profession. For example, Christian pre-med students are willing to consider practicing medicine overseas as medical missionaries or serving in under-resourced rural or urban areas in our own country because they are concerned with the unique opportunities that can come through physical healing in the name of Christ. Students majoring in engineering consider taking their training to places around the world that do not yet have clean water or basic infrastructure to dramatically improve the quality of life for those served and to open up doors for the gospel. Students heading into the business world concentrate on how they can buy, sell, and manufacture with integrity and how they can maximize their earnings to give to others. The examples are endless, but they are united by the fact that treasure in heaven holds higher value than any reward this world can offer.

Students who are confident that God will provide for them today and tomorrow have genuine peace about everything from their midterm and final exams to their future direction. They stand out from their peers who are constantly complaining about how stressed out they are. This peacefulness attracts attention in a positive way and provides opportunities to testify for Christ. Trusting in God's provision, these students carefully manage their time to have space for adequate rest and healthy living, leaving ample margin in their lives for serving others. They do not overcommit because they know that their overcommitment is not what provides for them. Sundays are special Sabbath days for corporate worship, meals together, activities that renew and energize, and time spent in purposeful conversation with each other.

Students who live this way genuinely flourish. May we all, students and workers of all types, greatly glorify God through our God-honoring work and rest!

# Acknowledgments

THE SERIES Questions for Restless Minds is produced by the Christ on Campus Initiative, under the stewardship of the editorial board of D. A. Carson (senior editor), Douglas Sweeney, Graham Cole, Dana Harris, Thomas McCall, Geoffrey Fulkerson, and Scott Manetsch. The editorial board recognizes with gratitude the many outstanding evangelical authors who have contributed to this series, as well as the sponsorship of Trinity Evangelical Divinity School (Deerfield, Illinois), and the financial support of the MAC Foundation and the Carl F. H. Henry Center for Theological Understanding. The editors also wish to thank Christopher Gow, who created the study questions accompanying each book, and Todd Hains, our editor at Lexham Press. May God alone receive the glory for this endeavor!

# Study Guide Questions

1. Why do you think busyness is so common in our culture? Do you think Christians struggle with busyness?

2. Sallade names three "errors" at the core of our culture's approach to work—what are they?

3. Why is work good? What is good about work?

4. Sallade argues that when Christians find our identity in Christ, we are able to rest both "physically and emotionally." What do you think she means by this?

5. What lesson can Christians learn from the manna-gathering practices of the Israelites?

6. How does the Bible define success?

7. What would it look like for you to carve out time for Sabbath rest? (See "For Further Reading" for helpful resources.)

# For Further Reading

Baab, Lynne. *Sabbath Keeping: Finding Freedoms in the Rhythms of Rest.* IVP, 2005.

The author shares her story of learning about the importance of Sabbath-keeping. She shares many testimonials about the benefits of observing the Sabbath as well as many practical tips about how to use the Sabbath for various stages of life and life-circumstances.

Crouch, Andy. *Culture Making: Recovering Our Creative Calling.* IVP, 2008.

This book defines the term "culture" and evaluates the vocabulary that has arisen around the term. It then describes how Scripture writes about the story of culture from beginning to end. Along the way, Crouch teaches how Christians today can participate in culture-making and renewing through our callings in our particular vocations. He urges Christians to join with God in his work of redeeming culture.

Dawn, Marva. *Keeping the Sabbath Wholly: Ceasing, Resting, Embracing, Feasting.* Eerdmans, 1989.

A book to teach and inspire Christians about the practice of Sabbath-keeping, rooted in Scriptures and lessons from Jewish practice. Dawn explains the joy and wholeness to be found in life when we cease from work, embrace other people, and feast in worship with other believers. She makes the case that we will flourish when we intentionally set aside our productivity and our striving and rest in God's abundant provision by observing the Sabbath.

——. *In the Beginning, God: Creation, Culture, and the Spiritual Life.* IVP, 2009.

Dawn creatively sets forth the Genesis creation account in a liturgical framework with the hope that the reader would use this portion of Scripture not just for information about our world, but also for worship. It has short chapters on a variety of topics that the opening pages of Scripture introduce, from taking care of the environment to working for justice to keeping the Sabbath.

Guinness, Os. *The Call: Finding and Fulfilling the Central Purpose of Your Life.* Thomas Nelson, 2003.

Guinness traces how people have understood "calling" throughout church history. There are helpful chapters on choosing one's vocational path.

Piper, John. *Don't Waste Your Life*. Crossway, 2003.

> Piper practically shows Christians how the culture of the day pushes us to live for comfort, leisure, and pleasure. He calls Christians to move away from such selfish pursuits and live instead for the glory of God. From Scripture and his own personal journey, he shows what it means to live for God's glory, and he applies this to our jobs, involvement with missions, illnesses, and stewardship of resources.

———. "Resources on Work & Vocation." http://www.desiringgod.org/ResourceLibrary/TopicIndex/6_Work_and_Vocation/.

> John Piper's website includes many relevant sermons and articles under the topic of work and vocation. I especially recommend the sermons "Why God Wills Work" and "Do Not Labor for the Food that Perishes."

Ryken, Leland. *Redeeming the Time: A Christian Approach to Work and Leisure*. Baker, 1995.

> This book defines the nature of work and leisure. It discusses historical attitudes about both of these realms of human experience through history, particularly focused on the Reformers and the Puritans. It sets forth a biblical understanding of work and rest, tracing both topics through the Scriptures.

Twenge, Jean M. *Generation Me: Why Today's Young Americans Are More Confident, Assertive, Entitled—and More Miserable Than Ever Before.* Free Press, 2007.

A very helpful, secular description of the newest generation (which she distinguishes from Gen X or Gen Y and calls "Gen Me"). It thoughtfully and entertainingly points out what this generation (youth to age thirty-five) is like and what in our culture has caused them to be that way. Twenge also offers advice on how to relate to this generation.

Welch, Edward T. *Running Scared: Fear, Worry, and the God of Rest.* New Growth, 2007.

A wonderful book of biblical theology that addresses all kinds of fears, anxieties, and desires for control. Welch explains these fears and the beliefs that cause them. He then applies the truths of Scripture to specific categories of our fears, including our money and possessions; fear of other people and their judgments; and fear of pain, death, and future judgment. He concludes with chapters on what it means for God to promise his followers peace.

# Notes

1. For an introduction to the topic, see articles and podcasts from the 2008 InterVarsity Graduate and Faculty Ministries conference on human flourishing at https://gfm.intervarsity.org/resources/following -christ-2008-conference-audio.

2. Quoted in Miroslav Volf, "God, Justice, and Love: The Grounds for Human Flourishing," *Books and Culture: A Christian Review* (January/February 2009): 1.

3. Certainly, there are many characteristics of student life and university policies today that could be discussed as contributing to a lack of flourishing besides busyness. For example, thoughtful critiques of coed dorm living and the sexual practices it encourages can be found in Vigen Guroian, *Rallying the Really Human Things: Moral Imagination in Politics, Literature, and Everyday Life* (ISI Books, 2005), 133–59. I think also of the widespread problem of binge drinking. The list could go on.

4.    David Brooks, "The Organization Kid," *The Atlantic Monthly* (April 2001): 40.

5.    For example, here is a report from a 2002 Princeton alumni magazine (and trends have not changed): "The number of students using Princeton's counseling center has climbed 30 percent in the last two years, according to clinical psychologist Marvin H. Geller. ... Last year Geller's staff met with 1,100 students with problems ranging from the situational, such as dealing with their parents' divorce or a death in the family, to serious mental illness including severe depression, anxiety disorder, and bipolar disorder. In the year ending June 30, 2001, the last year for which figures were available, 276 Princeton students were referred by the counseling center to psychiatrists, a 46 percent increase over the previous year, and two-thirds of those students were placed on medication. About 40 percent of all Princeton undergraduates use the counseling center at some point." Kathryn Federici Greenwood, "When College Life Overwhelms," *Princeton Alumni Weekly* (December 4, 2002).

6.    Kathryn Federici Greenwood, "The Pursuit of Perfection," *Princeton Alumni Weekly* (June 5, 2002): 16.

7.    David Brooks, "The Organization Kid," *The Atlantic Monthly* (April 2001): 41.

8.  Sara Rimer, "For Girls, It's Be Yourself, and Be Perfect, Too" (*New York Times*, April 1, 2007) archived at https://www.nytimes.com/2007/04/01/education/01girls.html?_r=1&pagewanted=print.

9.  Merrell Noden, "Admission Obsession," *Princeton Alumni Weekly* (December 12, 2007): 21.

10. "In 2003, Swarthmore rejected 62% of applicants with a perfect 800 verbal SAT score and 58% of students with a perfect 800 Math score. In the same year, Notre Dame rejected 39% of high school valedictorians who applied. Public universities have become more discerning as well. In 2004, the majority of freshmen at the University of Wisconsin graduated in the top 10% of their high school class. ... San Diego State, where I teach, used to be a party school almost anyone could get into, but these days, the average undergraduate earned a 3.5 GPA in high school and scored around the 80th percentile on their SAT's." Jean M. Twenge, *Generation Me* (Simon and Schuster, 2006), 116–17.

11. Merrell Noden, "Admission Obsession," *Princeton Alumni Weekly* (December 12, 2007): 22.

12. Twenge, *Generation Me*, 118.

13. And for the most part, I have not met many Christian students who live much differently. Christian students seem to struggle just as much

as non-Christian students with stress, anxiety, and depression. I do not think most yet know how being a Christian should affect how they pick their courses and their major, how they study, and how they manage their time. They have not yet realized how the gospel can release them from the pressure cooker environment they live in every day.

14. Dorothy Sayers, "Why Work" (an address she delivered in Eastbourne on April 23, 1942), https://centerforfaithandwork.com/article/why-work-dorothy-sayers.

15. John Piper, *Don't Waste Your Life* (Crossway, 2003), 139.

16. Piper, *Don't Waste Your Life,* 140–41.

17. I learned the following insights from pastor Timothy Keller. A sermon in which Keller teaches on this topic is available at the Redeemer Presbyterian Church website (www.redeemer.com). The sermon is titled "Made for Stewardship" and was preached October 22, 2002.

18. This struggle is made more intense by the fact that education separates out practical life matters and domestic arts for people to learn on their own. So students come to college and graduate with widely varying abilities to do such basic things such as cook, manage money, clean a home, etc. There is the same void in experience with caring for small

children or understanding basic things about childhood development, which is why the transition to parenting is such a jolt these days. Usually family background is what determines preparedness or lack thereof in these matters. I mention this because campus ministries and local churches can serve students by helping to give them a more holistic experience of life. For example, I continually urge college students to serve in the nursery to fill a constant need and also to learn about infant care along the way.

19. I also learned this from pastor Tim Keller. This sermon was titled "Work and Rest" and was preached March 23, 2003. It can be found on the Redeemer Presbyterian Church website, www.redeemer.com.

20. Os Guinness, *The Call: Finding and Fulfilling the Central Purpose of Your Life* (Thomas Nelson, 2003), 65.

21. For example, see Gustav Wingren, *Luther on Vocation* (Muhlenberg, 1957) or Martin Luther, *The Freedom of a Christian*, ed. Harold Grimm (Fortress, 1957).

22. There are of course other metaphors in Scripture that further define our relationship to God in Christ. For example, "sons through adoption" (Rom 8) and "friends of Christ" (the Farewell Dis-

course in John). We certainly need to keep these in balance with "slave."

23. For more on this topic, read Andy Crouch's excellent book *Culture Making: Recovering Our Creative Calling* (IVP, 2008).

24. A sermon by D. A. Carson on this parable is available at https://s3.amazonaws.com/tgc-documents/carson/2009_how_should_we_wait_for_Jesus.pdf.

25. John E. Smith, Harry S. Stout, Kenneth P. Minkema, eds., *A Jonathan Edwards Reader* (Yale University Press, 1995), 244.

26. Edward T. Welch, *Running Scared: Fear, Worry, and the God of Rest* (New Growth, 2007), 77.

27. Welch, *Running Scared,* 65.

28. Marva Dawn, *Keeping the Sabbath Wholly: Ceasing, Resting, Embracing, Feasting* (Eerdmans, 1989), 24.

29. Dawn, *Keeping the Sabbath Wholly,* 15.

30. I am grateful to Dr. Lawson Younger for teaching us the following lessons.

**LEXHAM PRESS**

QUESTIONS FOR RESTLESS MINDS

—

# CLARIFYING ANSWERS ON QUESTIONS FOR RESTLESS MINDS

**Series Editor: D. A. Carson**

The Questions for Restless Minds series applies God's word to today's issues. Each short book faces tough questions honestly and clearly, so you can think wisely, act with conviction, and become more like Christ.

**Learn more at lexhampress.com/questions**

Printed in the United States
by Baker & Taylor Publisher Services